A
Listener's Guide to
Preaching

A Listener's Guide to Preaching

William D. Thompson

ABINGDON PRESS ♪ Nashville New York

A LISTENER'S GUIDE TO PREACHING

Copyright © 1966 by Abingdon Press

Library of Congress Catalog Card Number: 66-14996

SET UP, PRINTED, AND BOUND BY THE
PARTHENON PRESS, AT NASHVILLE,
TENNESSEE, UNITED STATES OF AMERICA

TO EUTYCHUS *
the church's first recorded sermon-sleeper
and his innumerable descendants

Acts 20:7-12

A Word from the Author

If you go to church with some regularity, you hear a good deal of preaching. Whether you enjoy it or just endure it, you may not have given it a great deal of thought—how it came to be a part of public worship, for example, or precisely what it is supposed to accomplish.

In the last few years, the church's leading thinkers have been thinking and writing a lot about preaching. Partly because they are trying to reconstruct the life of the New Testament church with the greatest possible accuracy and partly because they are concerned about the effectiveness of preaching in today's world, they have come up with some insights that have tremendous significance for Christian preaching everywhere. At the same time, researchers in the behavioral sciences have discovered principles and techniques that help us understand the dynamics of communication—what happens when people talk to each other.

It is very nice for us specialists to carry on our research, to dispute fine points in our scholarly journals, and to read papers at each other in our convention meetings; but you who listen to preaching every Sunday are, after all, pretty important people in the whole process, too. By your response to the preaching, you ultimately determine its effectiveness.

Two convictions emerge from the current research in preaching which I think are worth your attention: one is that laymen share with their minister the responsibility for good preaching; the other is that laymen can be better Christians by learning how to be better listeners. I have been privileged to see a number of laymen come to share these convictions, to increase their enjoyment in going to church, and to lead more fruitful Christian lives as a result.

I offer this "listener's guide" with the hope that you too may find renewed means of Christian growth through preaching.

Contents

Contents

1

What Is Preaching?

BY WAY OF DEFINITION

"Preaching" is a word we shall use a great deal. It is hard for me to know just what you think about when you see it. If you worship regularly in a huge cathedral on the city's boulevard, you probably hear one kind of preaching. If you find your way to a cement-block basement church and sing to the accompaniment of piano and assorted brass instruments, you probably hear a different kind of preaching. Your church may be in a city neighborhood, or small town, or at a cornfield's

edge. The preaching to which you listen may not even be in a church; it may be in a hospital chapel, a prison cellblock, or in someone's living room. Your preacher may wear embroidered liturgical vestments, a simple Geneva collar, a dark business suit, or an open-neck white shirt. His language may reflect years of scholarly pursuit in Harvard's

Widener Library or hasty reading snatched in a city bus while commuting to evening classes in a Bible school. His sermons may abound with references to the lives of medieval saints, with quotations from offbeat poets of Greenwich Village or Paris, with dramatic personal experiences, or with one Bible verse after another. He may exhort you, comfort you, teach you, challenge you, berate you, compliment you, plead with you, bore you, titillate you, or inspire you. He may be fat or skinny, tall or short, handsome or ugly, bronzed or pale, raucous or somnolent, brilliant or dull, rich or poor. Ultimately, none of this matters. For a time each week he is a *preacher*. And though you will see your own church and hear your own

13

preacher when you encounter the word "preaching," you may be sure that you and I understand

roughly the same reality when the word appears. The reality is this—that every Christian preacher who fulfills his calling has a word from the Lord for you.

Simple, isn't it? So simple is it that we sometimes miss it completely.

Another word you will see often is "sermon." The very latest Merriam-Webster Dictionary lists as a secondary meaning "an annoying harangue." Well, if that is how some people feel about preaching, we'll just have to live with it. Sermon has another strike against it; it is a word which never appears in the Bible. Somewhere a few centuries back it wormed its way into common parlance from the same Latin word that gave us "series"—a joining together of a number of things. Sermon has no intrinsic, religious significance except what we ascribe to it as a matter of usage. It is so well-fixed in our language, however, that we will use it interchangeably with preaching and also as the product of the preacher.

PREACHING TODAY

Recently I appeared as a guest on a radio interview show and was asked about the importance of preaching in today's churches. The host, an active Christian layman, wondered aloud if people really take the sermon seriously these days. I told him that preachers frequently wonder the same thing!

The question isn't a new one, of course. Some of the most eloquent passages in the Old Testament reflect the bewilderment of a prophet at people's coldness to the Word of God. As long ago as

1897 a United States Supreme Court Justice summarized for an audience of theological students
the attitude many people of his day held.

We hear much today about the decay of the pulpit . . . you might be led to believe that it was an
institution fit only for semi-civilized times, and now
slowly passing out of existence. . . . That while then
(in the good old days) society rested and depended
on the pulpit, now the world finds that it is getting
along very well without often consulting it, and ere
long will dispense with it altogether.

The world has not yet dispensed with the pulpit, but in every generation there are those who
scoff at preaching, who merely endure it, or who
listen with considerable reluctance and suspicion.

Further darkening the name of preaching are
the psychologists who offer convincing evidence
that the speaker-audience relationship produces the
least efficient learning. They tell us that a discussion group is a better way to learn, or a sound film-
strip, or motion pictures. Later on, you will be
reading about some experiments I have done with
groups of lay people discussing the Sunday sermon. Sometimes the results make me wonder too
about the efficiency of preaching for getting ideas
across!

If it is not learning that the sermon is supposed to produce, but emotion of some sort, modern means of communication can do that more efficiently also. Think of the power of the motion picture to send chills up and down your spine, or to send tears coursing down your popcorn-treated cheeks, or to make you rise from your TV chair in righteous indignation at the injustice you see pictured on the world news roundup.

But, you say, preaching isn't limited to teaching or arousing emotion. It is supposed to move people, to change their behavior. All right, let's look at that one too. Who are the most powerful changers-of-behavior today? The wizards of the American advertising industry are—unquestionably. Their multimillion-dollar industry is built on their proven ability to control your buying habits. If you don't believe it, ask yourself why you bought that particular brand of toothpaste last week, or that hair dressing, or that variety of cereal. Unless you are part of that small, sophisticated minority of nonconformists who own neither TV nor radio and who never read advertisements, you responded effortlessly to the clever manipulation of a skilled copywriter who tapped your weak spot and made you buy. How clumsy is the preacher by comparison! Already medical science has discovered pills to calm us down and pep us up. We have all read the predictions of researchers who tell us that within twenty years drugs will be so highly de-

veloped that a skilled physician can control human behavior to a degree now beyond imagining.

Pity the poor preacher who has to compete with the movie magnate, the mass media, and the medicine man!

Part of the confusion about the value of preaching arises from a misunderstanding of what it is.

WHAT A SERMON IS *NOT*

1. A sermon is not a solo performance. In our entertainment-dominated culture it is very easy for us to think of the minister as a performer. Look at the similarities: he stands alone before an audience, perhaps illuminated by carefully concealed lighting; he may wear liturgical vestments or a flowing black robe—certainly he is neatly dressed and clean-shaven; he is expected to deliver his lines with a cultivated diction and an air of confidence;

he is generally available to the audience following the service to receive their congratulations.

To think of him as an actor or entertainer is of course a tragic mistake. However mistaken some preachers may be in conveying this impression is quite beside the point. In his deepest awareness—and yours—his presence in a Christian pulpit means far more than the appearance of a skilled actor playing to a devoted audience.

2. A sermon is not a commentary on current events. You may take a strong stand on either side of the debate that is raging today about the role of the pulpit in politics. One side says that preachers should not deal with political and economic questions; the other says with equal conviction that the church must speak out on all human problems of pressing concern. Thoughtful persons on both sides, however, concede that the congregation whose total sermonic diet consists of political essays is likely to die of spiritual malnutrition. These same persons know too that faith that has real depth helps the Christian to see right and wrong in sharp focus and compels him to speak out against injustice.

The real question is not whether preaching deals with social issues; it is whether its attention to public affairs is its *only* concern. Don't mistake the preacher's allusions to some current social problem as "meddling in politics." Don't, on the other hand, feel that he has failed his purpose if he doesn't offer analyses and solutions for all the world's ills. He may comment on current events, but his ultimate goal is far more important.

3. A sermon is not a theological or biblical lecture. It may sound like it sometimes. You may wend your way home after church, your head reeling with quotations from Tillich or Carnell or Küng. You may scratch your head over such strange words as *agape,* existentialism, or evangelicalism. Your preacher may feel that it is important to use these words in his sermons because they deal with significant ideas. If he is wise, he certainly tries to explain them. But even then you may miss their meaning because the words themselves scare you.

On the other hand, you may feel that you have not heard a real sermon unless it *was* in the nature of a lecture. The preacher's vocabulary of theological words or obscure biblical allusions impresses you. You rather like his discourses about ancient times or great social movements. It is precisely when he speaks in a purely objective fashion —lecture style—about principles, events, and ideas, that it is *not* preaching.

21

4. A sermon is not a lesson in Christian living. "It isn't?" you may exclaim. "Why, that's what I have always expected of preaching. You mean the sermon isn't supposed to give me guidance in my everyday life?"

Certainly, most sermons include a great many ideas and illustrations which are designed to teach you ways and means of talking and acting like a Christian. My own attempts at living a Christian life have been made more fruitful by the preaching on Christian living which I have heard. My rather bald assertion that instruction in Christian living is not the object of preaching is made in terms of *ultimate* objective. Moral instruction may be *part* of the preaching ministry, but is not its entire goal.

What then *is* preaching supposed to accomplish?

WHAT A SERMON *IS*

Understanding what a sermon *is* supposed to do has to begin with understanding something about God. You may know a great deal about him or very little. The thing that is most important to know is that he is desperately eager to make himself known to you. You may remember that in the Garden of Eden story God had some words with

Adam and Eve. That ancient biblical account marked the beginning of God's attempt to communicate with people. It is this "word" that is equated in the Bible with God's own being—his personality. One of the Gospel writers wrote, "In the beginning was the Word, and the Word was with God, and the Word was God" (John 1:1). This is another way of saying that right from the start of creation God was trying to make himself known. It is only upon this foundation that we can understand anything about preaching or listening to the Word of God.

How God attempted to make his Word known to people is, of course, the story of the Bible. The Old Testament's pages are checkered with success and failure. The New Testament tells of the coming of Christ, in whom God revealed himself most completely. Take a careful look at John 1:14: "And the Word became flesh and dwelt among us, full of grace and truth; we have beheld his glory, glory as of the only Son from the Father." It is obvious that God had decided to transform his Word into a human being, Jesus Christ. The theologians tell us that Christ became the "revealed Word."

As a matter of fact, the revealed Word stands for more than just the person we identify as Christ.

23

We can think of this Word more accurately as the Christ-event, that is, as the entire story of Christ; his birth, life, death, resurrection, and ascension. In all that he did and said, Christ was communicating God's desire to make himself known—his love for people and his yearning to have them live according to his way.

The recording of this story in the Bible is a second way we can think of the Word. We sometimes call the Bible the Word of God. And so it is. It is not a Word that is different from Jesus Christ; it is a different form in which the same Word comes to us. Look for a moment at the book of Acts as it describes the church at Beroea: "They received the word with all eagerness, examining the scriptures daily to see if these things were so" (Acts 17:11). This verse suggests that the Word comes to us in a written form, too. Just as Jesus Christ is the revealed Word, so the Bible is the written Word.

There is a third form of the Word—the form in which we are most interested right now. In attempting to explain to the church at Rome just how people can become Christians, Paul wrote, "The word is near you, on your lips and in your heart (that is, the word of faith which we preach). . . . So faith comes from what is heard, and what is heard comes by the preaching of Christ" (Rom. 10:8, 17). There it is. You have faith in Christ because of what you have heard about him. A preacher, perhaps several of them, proclaimed the good news in your hearing, and you responded by committing your life to Christ. It was in preaching —the proclaimed Word—that the Word of God really got through to you.

What *is* a sermon then? It is the Word of God (Jesus Christ) who has been revealed in the pages of the written Word (the Bible) coming to the hearing of people by the proclamation of the Word (preaching). To put it another way, the preaching of the Word is a divine event by which God makes himself known in the person of his Son, Jesus Christ, according to the witness of the Bible. Preaching is God himself at work, confronting mankind anew.

Do you see why preaching cannot possibly be merely a lesson in Christian living? Unless you confront the living Christ in the sermon and re-order your life because you sense his claim on you, you have simply heard some good advice from a nice man. Do you see why a sermon cannot be a theological or biblical lecture, or a commentary on current events, or a solo performance? Preaching is God revealing himself, reaching out to you,

25

calling you to respond—not man talking about God or any other topic, for that matter.

Did you ever stop to think that Christianity is the only one of the world's great religions which views preaching in this way? Judaism employs rabbis who speak at Jewish services of worship. The Eastern religions are spread by lecturers. The animist religions are communicated by ritual and oral tradition. But nowhere on earth is any religion spread by anything like the preaching of the Word. Why is this?

One reason, as H. H. Farmer reminds us in his book *The Servant of the Word,* is that the coming of Christ is completely unique. It is nonrepeatable. It is conceivable that after many centuries of reflections some person or society might come up with something almost identical to Hinduism. If there had been no Christians, however, to tell about Christ's saving act at Calvary, the message would have been lost. No one could possibly cook up such a story. If preaching in some form should stop today, Christianity would wither and die.

Another reason is that, in God's plan, preaching is part of the divine, saving activity itself. John the Baptist introduced the ministry of Jesus by preaching in the wilderness. Then Jesus himself carried it on. "After John was arrested, Jesus came into

Galilee, preaching the gospel of God" (Mark 1:14). When Jesus' preaching ministry was over, his disciples took it up and passed it on to preachers of every generation—including our own. More accurately, the gift and responsibility for preaching was given to the church, whose task it is to complete the saving work begun by Christ.

The final reason that preaching and Christianity cannot be separated is that God has always insisted upon dealing with the people of his creation in a personal way. He is a person. He created us human beings as persons. It was in personal relationships that, through Jesus, he made himself known to the world. It is through the personal relationship of preacher and people that he communicates himself today.

"But I feel God's presence when I partake of Communion," you may object. "And, furthermore, in the Lord's Supper the drama of God making himself known in Christ becomes clearer than in any sermon." Certainly it may. Christ is communicated by acts of compassion too, such as your visiting a person who is ill, or by writing a check for a mission school. The mighty God has not limited himself exclusively to preaching to have his work accomplished. But these ways of communicating Christ are personal too. And preaching is intensely personal. Apart from the church's preaching, the beautiful act of Holy Communion would eventually degenerate into meaningless ritual. Without consistent, biblical preaching to give it meaning, the Christian hand outstretched in love falls limp into a humanitarian gesture.

Does all this mean, then, that every sermon must retell the story of Jesus on the cross? Of course not. It does mean that the context of Christian preaching is God's saving work in Christ. Just as the entire Bible makes sense solely in terms of this act, so also does preaching on other parts of the Bible. Christ's person and work are the reference point in any Christian sermon on, say, humility or stewardship or Christian unity. "In him, all things [including preaching] hold together" (Col. 1:17). The preacher is not limited to a narrow list of subjects, nor to a particular way of organizing his materials. The only real limitation in operation is his willingness to respond to the Holy Spirit's guidance and your ability to shoulder your responsibility for good listening.

2

Who Is Responsible for Preaching?

Every so often an article appears in a magazine for preachers, written by a layman. Its title is usually something like "How We Like Our Sermons" or "The Kind of Preaching Laymen Expect." I always enjoy reading them. In fact, I collect them. They are filled with good advice—ideas that appear in textbooks on preaching, but generally much more to the point. As a preacher myself, I always manage a wry and somewhat uncomfortable smile at their repeated insistence that sermons should be shorter!

As a seminary professor of preaching, I am frequently invited to supply vacant pulpits on Sundays. Much of the time, I get an earful from some layman on the failure of preachers in the pulpit. The vocabulary and intensity of emotion varies, but the story is about the same: the preacher talks over our heads, or preaches too loudly, or too softly,

or doesn't use enough illustrations, or speaks in a monotone, or what have you. They are probably right, too. I know. I hear half a dozen practice sermons during the week—not every one a bell ringer—and occasionally a poor sermon by a visiting preacher in our chapel service. I dislike poor preaching as much as the next fellow.

But something about these sermon critics—in church or in print—bothers me. Every last one of them puts the blame squarely on the preacher!

Listen to the title again, "How We Like Our Sermons." I get the impression that the writer is somewhat of a connoisseur of preaching; a self-appointed, semiprofessional critic who knows what he likes about preaching. One of the problems with him, however, is that he probably likes only what he knows. And this implies the other problem; he may forget that in real preaching the listener hears a fresh word from the Lord—a word he may dislike very much!

Even more disturbing about the person who places the entire responsibility for good preaching on the preacher is that he woefully misunderstands the church—its nature and its function. According to the New Testament, the church is not the minister at the head of a group of people. The church is the people, the "called-out ones," the members of Christ's body in the world. It was not until long after the New Testament had been written that a professional clergyman took on the sole responsibility for preaching.

PREACHING IN BIBLE TIMES

The first Christians, as you know, were Jews. After their conversion to Christianity, they had no reason to change their basic pattern of worship —only their interpretation of the Scriptures. Even the Gentile converts took over the rather informal synagogue worship in which the people sang psalms, prayed, read the Scriptures, and shared in interpreting them. Their only real ceremony centered around the fellowship meal and the Lord's Supper, but these were also related in their thinking to the Jewish tradition—the Passover meal. It did not occur to the very first Christians to delegate the responsibility for preaching or officiating in worship exclusively to one of their members. The entire church shared the responsibility.

Witnessing to non-Christians was the church's responsibility too. There was no membership committee, board of evangelism, or minister of visitation. Every Christian felt and exercised the high privilege of sharing his faith, whether in personal conversation or preaching on the street corner.

Exactly how this responsibility was shared is not quite clear, but we do know that some of the men in the congregation were elected as elders. Unless one of the apostles was visiting a congregation, the elders alternated in their leadership of worship. This simple sharing soon became more complex, however. Even within the time span of the New Testament writings, certain men were said to have the "gift" of preaching. At various places Paul speaks of their exercising gifts of "prophecy," "exhortation," and "teaching." We also read about bishops, deacons, and presbyters, though these designations seem to have more to do with gradations in administrative duties than with the kind of speaking they did.

It is in one of the last books of the New Testament to be written that we find evidence of a changing pattern of ministry. The author of I John calls upon his readers in the early churches to test the spirits to see whether they are of God; for many false prophets have gone out into the world. The situation which gave rise to this warning was that all kinds of people were beginning to ride the coattails of the increasingly popular Christian movement. A traveling preacher might show up in town one sunny afternoon and ask for board and lodging for a few days. In the glow and naïveté of their simple faith the church had accommodated many an enterprising lunkhead whose "preaching" was a sorry business indeed, perhaps even quite unchristian.

One clear implication of this warning is that the church had the responsibility for conserving Christian truth. God did not entrust his revelation to some oratorically gifted soul who was available to fill as many speaking engagements as he could drum up. The Old Testament Scriptures, the letters of Paul, Peter, and other apostles, and the biographical accounts of Jesus' life were the possession of the church. The normal life of the church involved the study and public reading of this material, and its interpretation by persons who shared in this community of concern.

Another implication is that any variation on this norm, such as the itinerant preacher, was subject to the examination and approval of the church. For the church to take responsibility for the validity and effectiveness of its preaching ministry was by no means new. This warning is significant because the church was entering the postapostolic period in which a somewhat more professional ministry would become prominent. The writer wanted the church to preserve its responsibility for preaching and sound doctrine.

PREACHING IN TODAY'S CHURCHES

We all know what has happened to the church in the last two thousand years or so. The church's professional ministry has become the dominant and determining factor in the church's work. Apart from tiny nonconforming groups like the Plymouth Brethren and somewhat larger groups like the Friends, the preaching and leadership of worship is carried on by the clergy. We cannot argue here the merits of this development, but we can say that at least one value has been lost; the congregation's sense of responsibility for the preaching of the Word.

The congregation does, of course, retain some sense of responsibility. In many Protestant denominations the congregation extends a "call" to the clergyman. It is quite likely that a pulpit committee has been prowling around the ecclesiastical landscape looking for a minister who shines in the pulpit. Before they set out, they probably know something of his administrative record, his educational background, and his family life. When he takes up his parish work, they support him with a place to live and a salary—perhaps give him a number of fringe benefits. They further fulfill their responsibility by worshiping more or less regularly, listening to his sermons as best they can, and participating in the life of the church.

But here the responsibility stops.

Take yourself, for example. Suppose your minister invited you into his study next Tuesday morning to help him prepare his sermon. "Why, that's what we're paying *him* to do," you might say. Suppose he were to suggest that you stay a half hour after church some Sunday morning to discuss the ideas of the sermon with some fellow churchgoers. You might respond somewhat more favorably unless your schedule would not permit. When you got there, however, you might feel a bit uncomfortable about criticizing the sermon. You would really feel you had been put on the spot if, in addition, he asked you to write a sentence which embodied the main idea of the sermon.

Why the negative reaction to participating so actively in the preaching aspect of the church's life?

The answer is simply that you have never done any of these things before, and you hesitate about the unknown. You have never participated because both clergy and laity have falsely assumed that preaching is the preacher's private domain. It is, too. In fact, preaching is one of the last remaining forms of public address in America which is not subject to challenge and discussion by listeners.

In a recent study by Ronald Parsons at the Institute for Advanced Pastoral Studies in Michigan, less than 10 percent of Detroit churchgoers sampled had ever discussed the sermon with their minister or expressed to him their ideas about preaching. Less than 5 percent had ever had any instruction in the purpose of preaching, or any help in becoming better sermon-listeners. Hardly anyone among the hundreds of persons who participated in the research thought of himself as anything but a purely passive receptacle into which the preacher pours religious ideas every Sunday morning.

Anyone who has studied with a brilliant and creative teacher knows the value of questioning, disagreeing, searching for the clarification of a word's meaning, jumping ahead to new ideas. The form which our worship services generally take precludes this overt participation, but it need not keep us from the other forms of participation which can transform preaching into a marvelously exciting experience.

If preaching is the responsibility of the entire congregation, how can the congregation implement it? What specifically should the preacher bring, and what should the congregation bring?

CONTRIBUTIONS OF CLERGY AND PEOPLE

To the moments on Sunday morning when he stands in the pulpit as a preacher, the minister brings first a sense of the calling of God, verified by the witness of the Holy Spirit in his innermost being and validated in his ordination by the church. Whether speaking words of comfort and assurance or challenging our cherished but sinful habits and attitudes, he knows that he is speaking God's Word both to the church and in its behalf.

He brings a lifetime of preparation, however young or old he is; several years of higher education, the reading of innumerable books, a store of experience inside and outside the church, a complex of personal relationships. He probably brings many hours of detailed study on the sermon topic for the day (hours we'll look at in the next chapter).

He also brings himself as a person. If he is really called of God and is carrying on his ministry in the power and wisdom of the Holy Spirit, he has given the wholeness of his personality to the church and specifically to the sermon. Just as God was in Jesus Christ, a person, to *be* his Word, so he has chosen a person, your minister, to *preach* his Word. It is through human personality that God reveals himself.

To the hearing of the sermon you bring your needs, felt or unfelt, recognized or unrecognized, admitted or denied. We all come to church out of a society of brokenness and estrangement. We all participate in this society too—in family affairs, community life, business and social relationships. We need to hear the reconciling Word of God.

You also bring your relationships. A happy, well-ordered family relationship, for example, means that you will hear a sermon on Joseph and his brothers somewhat differently from another person because you will have to experience the feeling of family estrangement vicariously. Your relationship to the community, whether withdrawn from its affairs or deeply involved in them, will affect your hearing of the Word. Your personal relationship to the preacher has a great deal more to do with your reception of his message than you probably realize.

In the same way that the preacher brings his resources to the pulpit, so you also bring your resources to the listening task. You have spent a lifetime storing up experiences, insights, wisdom, attitudes, interests, and information which color and enrich what you hear.

Perhaps the expectations you bring have as much to do with the effectiveness of the preaching as anything. If you have convinced yourself that the sermon will be boring, dull, and unprofitable, you are not likely to be disappointed. We will talk about this phase of your contribution to sermon-listening in chapter 4. Perhaps William Carey's dictum makes sense here: "Attempt great things for God; expect great things from God."

Who is responsible for preaching? *You* are! You

share the responsibility with a person whom God has called to stand in the pulpit and on whom he has laid a unique burden to preach. But if anything is clear about the teaching of the New Testament, it is that the *church* bears the responsibility for witnessing and teaching and healing. And *you* are the church!

3

What's in a Sermon?

If you are a parent whose daughter has toiled many painful hours at the piano to prepare for a recital, you comprise the most appreciative part of her audience. You know what she went through to be able to perform. If you are a surgeon, you can appreciate better than a lay person the skill it took to manage so fine a scar on the new patient you examine. If you laugh uproariously at a toastmaster's humor, you do so with double appreciation

if presiding over an important dinner meeting is
a task you once struggled through.

You may never be called upon to preach a sermon, but you may be able to participate in the
church's preaching ministry more creatively if you
learn a little something about the process of preparing a sermon. What goes into a sermon anyway?

The process of putting a sermon together is as
varied as the preachers who do it. Like an artist,
each man has his own technique. Certain elements,
however, are always involved at some time in each
preacher's work.

CHOOSING THE IDEAS

Every sermon is made up of ideas. They come to
the pew-sitters in all sorts of forms—statements,
questions, stories, and so on. But they are of two
different kinds, main ideas and supporting ideas.
First, we want to understand the main idea of the
sermon. Sometimes, of course, a poorly prepared
sermon lacks a main idea. It just rambles around,
never really going any place. The chances are,
though, that the preacher has thought out pretty
carefully what he wants the sermon to do.

One time he may preach a sermon to win converts. Perhaps he is conducting a preaching mis-

sion to which you and he have invited persons who are not Christians. He may know on a given Sunday that some uncommitted persons will be present. Whatever the occasion, he is preaching in the tradition of the apostles, medieval itinerant preachers, and frontier evangelists who proclaimed as their central idea that "God was in Christ reconciling the world to himself" (II Cor. 5:19). This kind of preaching is sometimes called "kerygmatic."

More often his main idea is to teach. He will dig into some unfamiliar passage in the Bible which has an important lesson God was trying to get across in an ancient day. Through a careful study of the passage and the forces which gave rise to it, he will add some information to your store of knowledge concerning God. Of course, neither he nor you will be satisfied with a batch of new facts. The point of the sermon is that this information will result in some change in your way of life. A teaching sermon, for example, might affirm that "Hosea's response to an unhappy marriage parallels God's endless patience and sets a standard in patience for us."

Still another purpose the main idea may have is to help you with some problem. This sermon may incidentally impart some new information, but its focus is more likely to be on knowledge you already have. The preacher's purpose is to recall a truth to which you are already committed and help you to apply it in a contemporary situation. This kind of sermon is sometimes called "therapeutic" because it is designed to heal, to encourage, to stimulate, to inspire, to motivate. The main idea of a sermon based on the twenty-third psalm, for example, might be: "The only real security in our uncertain world is the constancy of the Good Shepherd."

Many preachers feel that they are not being faithful to the wide variety of human need in their congregation unless they include two kinds of main ideas—or perhaps all three. They may have a multilevel purpose for one sermon, attempting to provide something for everyone. This kind of preaching presents some problems for the listener who is seeking the sermon's main idea, but your minister may do just this, and you ought to be aware of it.

How does a preacher choose his main idea? He may start from one of two places, the revelation of God or the needs of the people.

Many preachers choose their sermon topics by turning first to a Bible passage. It may be prescribed by ecclesiastical authority or reflect an interest he has taken in a biblical passage, idea, or character. He may be preaching a series of messages whose subjects are dictated by the Bible. Whatever the basis for selection, he sees his task in the light of the biblical material.

If on the other hand he starts with the people, he articulates your need first—your ignorance of a certain truth, your hesitation in facing up squarely to a moral issue, your lack of dedication to a Christian principle. He moves from this point into the Bible, where he finds a verse or personality or sequence of ideas which may help you.

Preachers sometimes debate about the right starting point. What really matters is not the starting point but the end product. If the revelation of God intersects with the needs of the people, the sermon has done its work.

So much for the main idea.

Sermons have *supporting* ideas too. You have probably heard that sermons are supposed to have three points. You may even feel that you are missing something if you can't remember them. The whole notion of supporting ideas in a sermon, however, is that they *support*—not that they stand up and call attention to themselves. Some excellent sermons have only two chief supporting ideas; others may have five or more. To complicate matters, each of these supporting ideas may require from two to ten subsidiary ideas. Good sermon-listening doesn't require that you remember them. To know what they do, however, may help you to be a better listener.

In trying to achieve a predetermined response from the congregation as a result of the total sermon, the preacher generally has two tasks: to prove or authenticate what he is saying and to clarify or illuminate it. If he is affirming an idea he has good reason to believe you reject or know nothing about, he must do something to prove his point. He may appeal to an authority you respect—the Bible or the opinion of a person you admire. He may engage your mind in a process of reasoning based on an assumption you hold. He may offer statistics. If on the other hand he feels that you believe in some truth, but that your belief is not strong enough to motivate you to action, his job is to make that idea vivid and compelling. To this end he tells a story concerning persons with whom you may identify yourself. He employs an analogy, paints a word picture, relates a personal experience.

The ideas of the sermon—main idea or supporting ideas—are the stuff of which the sermon is made. The preacher has worked hard to determine these ideas and is ready now for the second major step.

ARRANGING THE IDEAS

One of the ways the preacher puts ideas together arises from the material itself. Perhaps his text is "What does the Lord require of you but to do justice, and to love kindness, and to walk humbly with your God?" (Mic. 6:8). It's a pretty good bet that he will have three points; one for each of God's requirements. If the biblical passage is longer, such as Hebrews 11, he may deal in turn with the various persons who are said to have lived by faith—Abel, Enoch, Noah, Abraham, Isaac, Jacob, Joseph, Moses (let's hope that he doesn't have *eight* main points!), and the others. Out of the first psalm he might deal first with the blessed man (verses 1-3), and then the wicked man (verses 4-6). The variety with which the preacher can organize his ideas is staggering.

Added to all this variety which the biblical material itself makes possible is a second category of organizational methods; he may arrange his ideas in terms of the congregation's needs or interests. The problem-solution pattern is a popular one. The preacher poses a problem we all face, such as temptation. He defines it and illustrates it, and then presents the biblical solution to it—perhaps in terms of Paul's assurance to the Corinthians that God

48

will provide a way of escape. Still another method is the implicative or "cliff-hanger." A preacher might deliver a sermon on the first thirteen chapters of I Corinthians in which he asks, "What kind of a church communicates its faith?" The early chapters demonstrate that a church whose members display a divisive spirit cannot, nor can a church whose members get involved in sexual immorality, nor can one which resorts to the law courts to solve its internal conflicts, and so on. At the very end of the sermon the preacher concludes that only the church characterized by love (chapter 13) can truly communicate its faith.

These examples hardly begin to describe the vast resources upon which the preacher can draw to make his sermons spring to life. You are fortunate if the preacher you hear knows and uses skillfully his organizational tools. But there is something to be said too for the one whose sermons are pretty predictable. As a listener, you can tell where he is going almost before he begins and have that much more energy to concentrate on the sermon's substance and its relation to you.

To this point, the preacher has a pretty good idea of what he wants to say and in which order he will probably say it. His next job is to determine the exact words he will use.

PUTTING THE SERMON INTO WORDS

It is at this point that preachers probably differ most widely in their sermon preparation habits. I know one preacher who composes a complete manuscript eighteen months in advance! I know others who through a lifetime of preaching have never once put a single word of a sermon on a piece of paper.

The preacher who does not commit his sermon to writing generally works from some sort of outline. It may be written in fine detail and cover many pages. Billy Graham once told me that he begins his campaigns with this kind of outline, and gradually cuts its size until, after a week or so in the same city, his outline for a forty-minute sermon is a little card with half a dozen words on it. Some of the "outline preachers" don't put their sermon into words until they step into the pulpit and open their mouths. Others have preached it countless times to the books in their study or to empty pews. Some take their outlines into the pulpit; others memorize them.

The "manuscript preachers" prepare a multipage document, usually well in advance of the occasion for preaching. They may compose it on the typewriter, write it in longhand, or dictate it to a dictating machine or stenographer. Not every manuscript preacher takes his manuscript into the pulpit with him; he may memorize it or fix it so clearly in mind that he can deliver it quite smoothly.

Where do the words come from? To some men they seem to come as easily as breathing. Other men slave over their sermons with a dictionary of synonyms, a set of commentaries, and a file of illustrations. However easily the words may or may not come, they soon find their way into grammatical forms which reflect the personality of the preacher and (hopefully) the level of the congregation's comprehension. To make ideas vivid the preacher uses word pictures, adjusts his sentence length, explains, illustrates, and defines. Wording the sermon is one of his most demanding jobs.

Both complicating and illuminating his work at this point is a raft of current writing on the use of religious language. It is this task which in our day occupies the best theological minds in the world. Theologians and preachers are more deeply concerned than ever with ways of putting into modern language the ancient truths of the Bible.

DELIVERING THE SERMON

The moment comes to every preacher and to every congregation when the goods must be delivered. It is at the moment of delivery that the ideas find their target or drop dully to the church floor. Whatever the excellency or inadequacy of the preacher's literary and theological craftsmanship, he is judged by what he does in the pulpit.

What elements help him get his message across to you as he stands in the pulpit and delivers the Word of God?

One element is his body. To help him meet the stress of the preaching situation the body supplies him with increased secretion of his adrenalin glands. What he does with that excess energy is critical to his effectiveness. He uses gestures and movements to attract and sustain your attention, to help you understand the relative importance of an

idea, and to help you see and feel more deeply the thing he is talking about. At the same time, he is using this extra energy to summon to his memory the material he has prepared.

His voice is the other tool he uses to communicate his message. Probably without any specific planning on his part, his voice conveys something about his personality and his feeling concerning you or the matter at hand. In the seminary classroom we help every man evaluate his voice according to the traditional criteria of pitch, rate, volume, and quality. We also help him to evaluate the clarity of his articulation and the correctness of his pronunciation. Many seminaries use tape recorders, and a fortunate few are equipped with video tape machines to enable the budding preacher to see and hear himself as others see and hear him.

The process of preparing a sermon is a difficult, time-consuming, and rewarding one. Knowing how the preacher goes about it is one of the best ways to increase your listening efficiency. But there are some other ways too.

4

Preparing for the Sermon

How wonderful it would be to belong to a church in which the pulpit communication is excitingly complete every Sunday! We would all like to hear sermons which find their mark every time; which stir, inspire, and move us week after week. We would like to be part of a community which exemplifies the Christian faith at its best, partly as a result of good preaching and good listening.

Why is such a church so rare?

Poor preaching is part of the answer—but only part of it. The rest of it involves you, the listener. And your involvement begins with your preparation for listening.

Here are eight suggestions for preparing to listen to the sermon. You will profit from the preaching in direct proportion to the seriousness with which you follow them.

1. *Reflect deeply on the total meaning of preaching in your Christian growth.*

What is the meaning—the value—of Christian preaching anyway? Part of the answer lies in the value God himself places on it. God gave preaching to the church, not as a burden, but as a gift. It is a gift to be sought in prayer, both by clergy and laity; to be nourished by self-examination; and to be received with thanksgiving.

Whatever value preaching has as a means of Christian growth is "inside" the listener. Preaching has no value to the church or community as a kind of religious performance. There is no intrinsic merit in the words the preacher says or in the skill with which he says them. What really matters is your reception of them. Any sermon has value for you only as it awakens forgotten knowledge and resolutions; only as it helps you to see human relationships with keener insight; only as it gives you information about God and yourself which you may find useful; only as it focuses your eyes more clearly on God's greatness and goodness. In one sense, listening to a sermon is a learning process. Learning requires that something happen inside the learner.

The inside dimension is only part of the story, however. Whatever good is to come about, you see, is good which you will bring about. Having gotten inside you, the Word of God now has to move "outside" of you. When the sermon has really hit the bull's-eye, you become reconciled to someone from whom you were estranged; you resume your occupation with a heightened sense of its importance in God's plan; you rearrange your schedule to include prayer, community service, study, frequent worship.

2. *Determine to discover the relevance of the particular sermon for your life.*

Ideally, of course, the preacher should do this for you. He has taken the courses and read the books which equip him to be "relevant." But just between us, he doesn't connect *every* week, does he?

In that case, finding the relevance of the sermon becomes *your* job.

57

One way you can do this is to reaffirm your responsibility, as a member of God's family, for preaching. You may not be able to stand in the pulpit and do a better job, but you can say, "I won't allow this sermon to be a total waste." You can be sure that *something* being said is valuable. You are an adventuresome soul, and you determine to find the sermon's value.

Another action you can take is to identify yourself, your family, your church, or your community with some idea in the sermon. To yourself you can say, "Why, we're just like the people in that obscure Old Testament story, aren't we?" Find one solid idea in the sermon, even if it is not the elusive main idea, and make it your own.

You can certainly make your intention an object of prayer, either in your family group or in your private praying.

3. *Become familiar with biblical material and ideas—if possible, with the sermon text.*

I wish I could prove it, but I have a sneaking hunch that the more people know about the Bible, the better sermon-listeners they are. When the preacher is moving along lickety-cut about facing the future unafraid and says, "Now, we may not suffer the same result as Lot's wife, but . . ." he loses a lot of people. How are you to know that

Lot's wife turned into a pillar of salt because she looked back?

So the preacher is to blame?

Maybe. But maybe part of the blame lies with listeners whose Bibles are gathering dust and whose schedules are too full for regular Bible study.

You see, what we know about God is largely a matter of historical record. The Old Testament is a chronicle of God's various attempts at self-revelation and man's response. The New Testament centers around his final and finest revelation, Jesus Christ, and man's response to him. These writings provide the raw materials and the backdrop of all preaching. Just as current events in Washington make sense only in the light of American history, so does our life in the church (including listening to its preaching) make sense only when we know something about the church's history.

I have heard a lot of arguments for adult Christian education. I'd like to add another; it makes for profitable listening at sermon time.

One of the most interesting developments along this line is the emerging of lay groups who meet with their minister to study the sermon text before he prepares the sermon. The Rev. L. Ray Sells of the Warsaw (Indiana) Methodist Church wrote me about his experience.

Each person who attends is to have read the Scripture prior to coming, and to share his ideas and thoughts about the passage and its meaning. The preacher is responsible for providing background by way of exegetical work [1] to aid in understanding. From the discussion this prompts, notes are made of significant points or of the points where agreement and disagreement are reached. Usually the notes are in the form of questions or issues which must be further clarified if the sermon is to be relevant. This group also provides a basis for testing the clarity or, more truthfully stated,

---

[1] *Exegetical* is one of those long words preachers use to impress each other. It means that the preacher has studied the historical setting, read the passage in the Greek or Hebrew, and arrived at its basic meaning.

the nonclarity of our ideas. One feels more comfortable with an idea when it has been digested by others, and this digestion process creates a much clearer idea. I am "hooked" on this method. I shall never again approach preaching without this kind of process.

Obviously, not every pastor will engage in this kind of dialogue. He may never have thought of the idea, or he may have some objection to it. If you worship in a church in which the Scripture reading is prescribed for each Sunday, you may secure a copy of the book of readings (the lectionary) and read a week ahead. If the preacher doesn't use this system, he may be willing to announce a week ahead of time the basis for the next Sunday's sermon—perhaps in the parish bulletin or even from the pulpit.

Wherever pastor and people have tried this kind of cooperative sermon planning, they have managed to recapture some of the excitement of the early church and to see the sermon really live!

4. *Develop your listening skills.*

Listening, as we shall discover in the next chapter, is considerably more difficult than rolling off the proverbial log. All kinds of things happen to keep people from understanding each other. The philosophers, general semanticists, theologians, and psychologists have a delightful time analyzing these things. What is important here is that the people (1) understand some of the basic principles of listening, all of which are explicit or implicit in this book, and (2) practice these principles.

Courses in listening are popping up all over the academic landscape. People in offices, plants, shops and service clubs have suddenly discovered that they spend more time listening poorly than almost anything else except sleeping, and they are hiring teachers of listening. Universities are spending considerable research money to discover methods of teaching and learning listening.

When pew-sitters take the trouble to study and practice listening skills, sermons are likely to become pretty exciting.

5. *Remember that communication is a reciprocal activity.*

We are learning that real communication takes place between people only when they are sending signals to each other that both can understand. People communicate only when they reciprocate meanings—that is, when there is a real "give and take" between the persons talking and listening. A new academic discipline has emerged in recent years to help us understand just how this process works—"communication theory." Let's look at it.

Let's say that you are waiting for a committee meeting to begin. You are chatting amiably when you suddenly remember that you will need some chalk later in the meeting to put your report on the chalkboard. Since your friend Hector is seated near the table drawer in which the chalk is kept, you say, "Hector, will you please get some chalk for me out of that table drawer?" Graciously Hector opens the drawer, reaches in, grasps the chalk firmly, withdraws his hand, closes the drawer, and hands the chalk to you with a smile.

A communicative act has just occurred.

What happened?

It all began with an idea which we shall call the *source*. The idea was somewhere inside of you. We'll call you the *encoder*, because you had to put that idea into a code—a word—in order to make known to Hector what you wanted. The words you spoke we shall call the *message*. To get that message to him, you had to employ what we shall call a *channel*; you had to disturb the air between yourself and him, setting up sound waves. We shall call Hector the *receiver*—the target of your communicative effort. Hector's job was to act as *decoder*, that is, to translate that word "chalk" into a mental

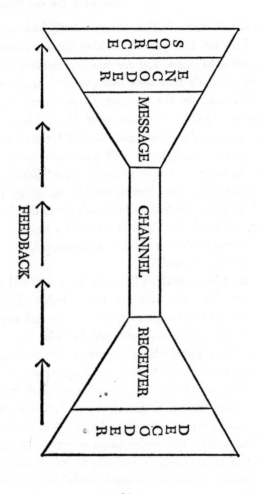

image which corresponds to the idea you started with. His response to your request—both the way he looked at you and the action he took in response to your request—is called *feedback*. In feeding back, Hector now becomes the source, and you the receiver.

This entire act, of course, took only a couple of seconds. Because it happens so often and with such great efficiency, you were not even aware of the processes involved. Nor may you be aware of the importance of knowing how this process works.

Let's consider how the communication cycle could have been broken. If, for example, you could not identify what was disturbing you but only had a vague feeling of needing something, the communication would have stopped at the *source*. Perhaps you knew what it was you wanted but could not think of the word to describe it. To be thinking, "Oh, what is that thingamajig I want?" would mean failure at the level of the *encoder*. Suppose you can encode the idea into the word "chalk" but something in your brain goes wrong and the *message* comes out, "Chive me the galk, please." If the room is noisy, the *channel* is clogged, and the message doesn't get through. Hector may be hard-of-hearing or occupied in conversation with someone else, and thus be unable to act as *receiver*. If Hector knows little English or has come from a village in Tahiti in which he has never seen chalk, he is not likely to act as a very good *decoder*. Even if the cycle is complete, but you get no response, the lack of *feedback* is crucial.

You can see, can't you, how easily the cycle of communication can be broken. And this is an extremely simple example. Think of how much more difficult it is for your preacher, who deals with abstract words and complicated ideas. In my first pastorate, an inner-city church in Chicago, I discovered that preaching about God as "Father" was the worst word I could choose for some of the young people. To them "Father" meant "that guy who comes home every couple of weeks and beats up my Mom." One boy said, "If God is like that, I hate him!"

What we have done so far is to look at the communication process as the psychologists describe it. Now, let's look at it theologically.

As encoder and decoder we are persons, human beings created by God, who know that we are persons. As persons, we have a deep concern for our own being. We know the dignity of being human. Further, we have lived through a wide variety of experiences. We value our being, our humanity, the meaning of our life.

As Reuel Howe reminds us in his excellent book *The Miracle of Dialogue,* this self-concern draws us into relationship with other persons because we need reassurance of our worth, and only other persons can provide it. It also separates us from other people, however, and makes it difficult for us to communicate with them. If our experience suggests, for example, that attempting to communicate with a minister may result in our being scolded or embarrassed, our need-to-be shuts off the possibility of such communication. This same self-concern profoundly affects our willingness to listen to ideas that challenge our spending practices, our attitudes toward other races, or our use of leisure time. We have formed certain postures and patterns of living in these areas, and they are now intimately bound up with our very being.

On the other hand, this need-to-be opens up the possibilities of communication. We encode and send messages which we have some reason to believe will result in our being understood and appreciated. We seek earnestly to receive and decode messages, say from a preacher, which may help us to understand ourselves and our place in God's will. We do all we can to keep the channel clear of noise and distractions that might hinder our being everything we are capable of being.

If preaching is to be genuine communication it must be reciprocal, or in Dr. Howe's term, "dialogical." In his words, "Dialogue is that address and response between persons in which there is a flow of meaning between them in spite of all the obstacles that normally would block the relationship." In communicative preaching, the preacher honestly brings to his encounter with you the meanings he finds in the Scriptures and in himself; you bring the meanings you have derived from Scripture and from life. In this encounter of meanings, real communication takes place.

What does this awareness of the communication process mean for the sermon-listener?

For one thing, it makes apparent what we already knew, that we sometimes fail to understand the sermon because the preacher brings a different set of meanings to it than we do. He may be very excited, for example, over what seems to you a rather fine point of theology because it means to him a satisfactory solution to a knotty question that had driven him to several hours' study. It doesn't mean anything at all to you, since it never bothered you—never touched your need-to-be.

Another implication of communication theory is that its very complexity (and I have hardly hinted at how complex it can be) guarantees its failure some of the time. If you expect too much of your preacher, or of yourself as a listener, you are sure to be disappointed. Don't expect him to score every time he gets up to bat. Don't expect yourself to remember every idea in every sermon.

Perhaps the most important result of knowing how communication works will occur when you consciously and deliberately bring your experiences into encounter with the ideas of the sermon. Listen to every sermon with the recurring question always at the forefront of your thinking, "What does that mean to me?"

6. *Listen in anticipation of sharing your new insights.*

Every college freshman who takes an education or orientation course learns about the learning retention curve. He may even participate in an experiment to demonstrate how rapidly people forget what they have heard. He will also discover that he can significantly increase his retention by talking about what he has just learned or writing it down. Somehow the very process of sharing your knowledge with someone nails it down in your own mind. There is real sense in the axiom, "If you really want to learn something, teach it to someone."

We are going to talk about ways to do this a bit later on. Let's just say here that listening which has the purpose of sharing is the best kind there is.

7. *Prepare your body to listen.*

Good listening requires energy. In his book *Listening and Speaking*, Ralph Nichols describes as one of the characteristics of good listeners "increased heart action, faster circulation of the blood, and even slightly increased bodily temperature." He goes on to say that the very word "attention" suggests a collection of tensions within the listener which are resolved only when the speaker's message is communicated.

Pew-sitters like you are pretty good judges of whether the preacher has your attention. When he doesn't, it is only natural to blame him. Perhaps much of the fault *is* his. Another possibility which may add to your inattentiveness, or even be at work all by itself, is your own energy level. If you have less sleep than you need on Saturday night, attention will be difficult to focus. If the Sunday morning routine at your home is interrupted, or if it is tension-filled or upsetting, your listening ability will be impaired.

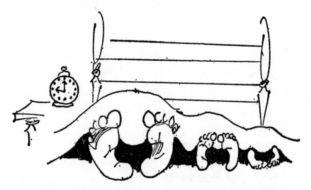

The solution is easy to prescribe, more difficult to carry out. Get to bed Saturday night in time to allow proper rest. Plan your Sunday morning routine so as to avoid unnecessary expenditure of energy.

8. *Enter fully into the total experience of worship.*

Whatever the form worship takes in your church, you gather for worship to sense the presence of God, to hear his Word, and to respond to him in obedience. No matter how complex or simple the pattern you follow, every element of the worship service is designed to facilitate this encounter with God. The prayers, the hymns, the giving of gifts, the quiet moments for prayer before the service, the use of symbols—all of these work to make up the totality of a divine-human meeting.

Most churches view the reenactment of the Last Supper as a sacrament, a means by which God uses human or physical means to communicate himself. Even for nonsacramental churches, the service of Communion is a special time in which God's presence is felt most deeply. The current renewal of biblical theology is helping us to understand preaching as a kind of sacrament in which God comes to men uniquely—through human words. Many Christian communions are restudying and restructuring their liturgies to restore the balance of "Word and sacrament" which characterized the New Testament church's worship.

I know you can't possibly fulfill these ideals all the time. I can't either. But knowing what elements make up good listening may go a long way to help.

AN ADDED WORD

One of the most helpful sermons your minister can ever preach is a sermon on the people's responsibility for good listening. The Bible is filled with texts which might open up this subject (an especially good one is the parable of the sower—Mark 4:1-20). If you request such a sermon in a spirit of helpful concern, he may find an opening in his preaching schedule for it. Certainly he will give your suggestion honest consideration.

5

Listening to the Sermon

If you worship every Sunday you may spend from ten to forty minutes a week listening to a sermon, in some churches even more. While listening to a sermon, unlike reading a magazine article, you cannot turn back the page to reread a sentence you may have missed. If you want to profit from what the preacher says, you must understand at the moment of delivery.

As I have tried to help people become better

listeners, I have discovered three obstacles over which they stumble. Let me put them in the words of the people themselves.

1. "I can't hear what the preacher is saying."

To get over this obstacle, you have three choices. The first is to sit closer to the preacher. Acoustics in the church are seldom perfect, and some preachers fail to adapt their voices to the room. If, in addition to that, your hearing is less than 100 percent, the only sensible thing to do is to sit where you can hear. Don't let a habit of sitting in a certain place keep you from hearing God's Word to you.

The second thing you may do, if changing your

seating position doesn't work, is to have your hearing tested by an audiologist and to take whatever steps he recommends. Hearing devices are available in a variety of prices, and many of them are almost undetectable, if that makes a difference to you. Some churches make available hearing devices which are connected to the public address system. Use one.

If the fault is entirely the preacher's, tell him so. He may be able to speak louder, or he can have the amplifying system adjusted, or can have one installed. Your telling him may be a favor to others in the congregation who for some reason do not wish to tell him.

2. "The preacher is just too dull."

The person who says this poses a more difficult

problem. He is really saying more about himself than he is about the preacher.

It may be true that his preacher does not have all the rhetorical and homiletical skills of the man who packs in crowds every Sunday in the big city church. He may even be extremely difficult to listen to, and the difficulty may be largely his fault. But to excuse oneself entirely from careful, creative listening on that basis is poor stewardship of one's God-given intellect.

The answer to this objection is twofold: the first is that you have a theological responsibility for good listening; the second, that in listening you have an opportunity for growth which comes to you in no other way. It was G. K. Chesterton, I think, who said that there is no such thing as an uninteresting subject; there are only uninterested people.

3. "I find it difficult to concentrate."

All kinds of things can happen to keep you from concentrating. Some of them happen outside your control; others happen inside you. Let's take a look at both of them.

According to Professor Ralph Nichols, probably America's chief authority on listening, the basic cause of difficulty in concentrating is our multidirectional orientation. By this he means that our lives are so complex—we have so many things to think about—that a wide variety of thoughts is constantly competing for our attention. Even in a quiet church sanctuary with a single stimulus—the preacher—we interweave our thoughts about

the sermon with worries about the roast, the brake linings, next Saturday's date, or the increased cost of living. The chief form this obstacle takes is "progressive tuning out." We tune out for a moment, then back in, and out again. We add progressively longer periods of time away from the sermon until its total effect is almost zero. How can we do all this in the short time the sermon takes?

Dr. Nichols reports some astonishing research in answer to that question. It is fairly well known that the average public speaker can get across somewhere between 100 and 200 words a minute. Slower than 100 words is too slow to sustain our attention more than a few minutes; faster than 200 pushes his speech into unintelligibility. What is less well known is that, depending largely on our intelligence, we can listen to between 400 and 700 words per minute. Theoretically, if a speaker could produce say 525 words a minute before an average audience without distortion, we could comprehend every word and idea!

What this means, obviously, is that we can listen accurately to everything the speaker says, comprehend it perfectly, and still have a great deal of time to do something else. What we do with that time determines how skillfully we listen! We may follow our thoughts down memory lane or off into the future. We may dwell upon the things that distract us; or we may exercise the skills that will make us good listeners.

Now let's look at three barriers to concentration in the light of this research.

BARRIERS TO CONCENTRATION

Distractions form the first barrier to concentration. You know what distracts you far better than I do. If you are an American female adult, you are probably distracted by the wearing apparel of another American female adult. If you are a teen-age boy, you may very well be distracted by a teen-age girl. You may be distracted by an airplane landing nearby, a fly preparing to land on the preacher's nose, a whooshing sound escaping from an ancient pipe organ, a draft or a blast of hot air. Distractions from good sermon-listening are legion.

"How can I ignore a jet breaking the sound barrier," you ask, "or a choir member who sneezes?" Obviously, you can't ignore every distraction. No one expects you to. The question is, How long does it take you to get back to the serious business of listening? The answer depends entirely on the seriousness with which you take it. If you get as deeply involved in the sermon as you should, you'll get back on the job within seconds.

Overstimulation is the second barrier to concentration. Have you ever found yourself mentally taking off on a word or idea you heard in the sermon? The preacher mentions communism as one of the influences at work to change the world. Immediately your mind flashes to the Berlin wall, to the sight of an escapee being shot as he scrambles over this barrier to freedom; you remember a vivid account of life in a Siberian concentration camp; you hear the rumble of tanks crawling into Budapest to crush the 1956 revolt. You follow wherever your previous associations lead you. By the time you have finished reacting emotionally to the word "communism" (which had nothing to do with the main point of the sermon anyway), you have lost the thread of the preacher's idea and are fair game for some distraction, or tangent-following, or some other emotion-stimulating word.

All of us have somewhere in our subconscious minds a list of words to which we react somewhat emotionally. Perhaps you become overstimulated by "fundamentalist," or "liberal," or "modernist," or "fair housing," or "myth," or "civil rights," or "ecumenical." When you hear that word, your blood boils, your temperature rises, you engage in a mental debate with someone who stands for what you don't like. And all the time you are doing that, you miss every good point the poor preacher is trying so hard to make.

The solution is to get those words up into your consciousness. Take a good look at them. Why do you react to them the way you do? Are they worth getting so excited about? Do you still feel as deeply about them as you once did? Have you really understood what the preacher is saying about them? Wouldn't it be a good idea to withhold evaluation of an idea or a word until you are sure you know enough about it to react to it honestly? Would it help to discuss this barrier with your minister?

I certainly don't advocate that you check your emotions at the church door every Sunday morning. I do say that letting yourself become over-stimulated by provocative words or controversial ideas is a good way to lose out on hearing the Word God may have for you in the sermon.

A variant on this barrier is "blacking out." I,

for example, am the world's worst weather listener. I can listen to the weather forecast at the end of a news broadcast and be totally unable to tell you what the man said. I have accommodated myself to the cultural dictum that requires us occasionally to talk about the weather, but I really haven't the vaguest interest in it. If I were a farmer or tugboat pilot or truck dispatcher, I would listen keenly. But I am none of these, and I simply turn my mind to another matter, ever so briefly, during the weather report.

You probably have a "blackout area" in sermon-listening. It may be the area of stewardship, by which is generally meant money. Perhaps you turn off the preacher when he begins to talk about Albert Schweitzer or some favorite person to whom he alludes far too often. Time was that a subject overstimulated you. You have now learned not to waste energy getting excited; you just snap the mental "off" switch.

Keeping the switch on the "off" position is yet another variant. Most of us are pretty skillful at this. We tune out the sermon near the beginning and stay out. Not wanting to reveal our inattention, however, we make it appear that we are listening—we "fake attention." We retreat to our

own world of fantasy while giving the impression of listening by a physical posture of attentiveness.

Tangent-following is the third barrier to concentration. It is a close cousin to the first two barriers, distraction and overstimulation. The prime difference is that it grows not out of some external stimulus or an emotion-laden word, but out of some perfectly good and helpful thing the preacher says. You may have a friend to whom something the preacher says applies, and you begin thinking about that person. You may hear an unfamiliar word about which you begin to think. "Now I've heard of Obadiah. Is he in the Old or New Testament? He was the fellow whose wife gave him such a hard time. No, that was Hosea. Maybe he was one of the Judges. I wish the preacher would identify those unfamiliar names. Maybe he. . . ." And while you are following a tangent, the sermon has turned a corner to deal with a question that really interests you. But you, you tangent-follower, missed it!

It is entirely possible, of course, that the Holy Spirit may lead you off on a tangent which is far more helpful to you than anything the preacher might say. If that happens, so be it! I suspect, however, that such an occurrence is the exception, not the rule.

The remedy for the tangent-follower is, in one sense, the remedy for all the ills that beset the listener to preaching. Here are five ingredients of good listening. Digest them well.

INGREDIENTS OF GOOD LISTENING

1. *Listen for main ideas,* especially the single main idea that ties the entire sermon together. You may remember from chapter 3 that the substance of the sermon is composed of ideas and supporting material. As you gain practice in listening, you will learn to separate the ideas—the assertions— from the illustrative material. One of the hazards to good listening is precisely at this point. Listeners frequently get carried away with a striking illustration and forget the point of the sermon. They sometimes perceive a relatively unimportant idea and appropriate that idea for themselves. To do so is not, of course, entirely bad. In fact, I have already suggested that you should try to get a hold on one idea and make it your own. What I am suggesting now is that finding the sermon's main idea is better than singling out a random idea.

Let me suggest a way to arrive at the sermon's main idea. Professor Henry B. Adams of the San Francisco Theological Seminary devised this technique, and I have used it with considerable success. It involves writing a series of three sentences at the conclusion of a sermon. The first sentence is in question form: To what human problem or situation did this sermon address itself? You might write, "Do we have all the strength we need to meet temptation?" The second sentence is a statement which sums up or epitomizes the answer to that question such as, "Watching and praying comprise Jesus' formula for overcoming temptation." The third sentence states the response which the sermon calls for, in the form of an invitation: "Let us restructure our lives to handle our temptations according to Christ's pattern—using our common sense (watching) and God's power (praying)." Either the second or third sentence might be considered the main idea of the sermon. You may wish to write it out during the service or as soon as possible thereafter. Even forming the words on your lips helps to keep the idea in your mind.

The obvious difficulty with this method is that the preacher himself probably doesn't use any such pattern in his sermon preparation. My research suggests that even when he does, some listeners have difficulty writing these statements. Even so, the very attempt to put into your own words the preacher's ideas is a worthwhile project. Presumably, he does begin with some sense of need on your part. He almost certainly has a single idea he wants to get across. And he would not be preaching if he did not want you to respond in some way. However he may organize his material, you will find it challenging and helpful to analyze it in these terms.

A simpler method is used by Dr. Reuel Howe, director of the Institute for Advanced Pastoral Studies in Michigan and a pioneer in involving laymen in sermon discussion groups. He asks sermon listeners to put into words an answer to these questions: "What did this sermon say to you?" "What difference, if any, do you think the message will make in your life?" And perhaps, "What did the preacher do to help or hinder the communication?"

However you do it, listen for the main idea.

2. *Anticipate the speaker's next point.* Experiments in training listeners at the University of Minnesota suggest very strongly that trying to predict what the speaker is going to say is one of the best ways to utilize listening time. From the sermon's very start ask yourself, "What is the preacher getting at today? How is he likely to develop his next point?" If you guess correctly, you

are reinforcing your impressions—one of the best ways to retain information. If you guess incorrectly, you can compare what you thought he would say with what he actually said. Doing this is another excellent method of learning, comparison and contrast. Either way, you gain when you anticipate. And you have plenty of time to do it.

3. *Identify yourself with the sermon's ideas.* Try to see how you, your family, your church, and your community fit into the insights of the sermon. Ask, "Where would I have been had I been one of Jesus' followers near the garden of Gethsemane?" or "Is our church anything like the church at Ephesus?"

Remember that the sermon is a unique form of public speaking. God himself speaks through his Word as it is preached. He will not be heard, however, unless his people open their ears to hear him. To discern correctly and with insight the things God wants to say to the man in the next pew or to the church across town doesn't count. It is *you* God is trying to get through to!

4. *Review what you have heard.* Repetition is one of the most efficient forms of learning, as every teacher and parent knows. You are fortunate if the preacher employs intelligent and creative repetition

in the development of his ideas. Even if he doesn't, you can reap the benefits by repeating to yourself the ideas you have been listening to. During the few seconds between sentences, you have ample time to say to yourself, "The first two points were that God allowed Jesus to be tempted, and that he was tempted in the wilderness. Now here comes the third point."

You can recapitulate like that—in such a short time—because you do not have to form the ideas into words. Just as a whole host of pleasant associations pass through your mind when you suddenly spy an old friend across the street, so in a few seconds you can mentally pull together the ideas you have been listening to, in far less time than it would take you to put them into words.

5. *Put these principles to work in every listening situation.* In one of his lectures to businessmen on the values of listening training, Dr. Nichols notes that poor listeners universally avoid listening to difficult, expository material. Their choice of television shows is composed almost entirely of situation comedies. Any group of good listeners, on the other hand, has a generous proportion of persons who regularly watch documentaries, discussions, and interpretative newscasts.

Because we human beings are whole persons, not collections of isolated skills and interests, our proficiency in one area of life frequently carries over into other areas. It is manifestly impossible for you to develop into a really skillful sermon-listener in a vacuum. The degree to which you listen to serious, provocative material on radio and television, in community affairs, and in other areas of church life will affect profoundly your ability to hear God's Word with clarity. Similarly, the skills you may begin to gain in the context of sermon-listening will be reinforced by insightful listening elsewhere.

Listening to a sermon is an exciting and challenging task, if you will make it so. But there's a final task, and a final chapter to talk about it.

Here is the form Professor Adams uses to help people put the sermon's ideas into words. Why not use it the next time you hear a sermon?

WHAT THIS SERMON MEANS TO ME

A sermon is a mutual experience we all share, something that happens among us. Your understanding of the sermon will not be exactly like anyone else's, but it is an important part of the total meanings which make up the message today.

Try to digest the sermon into three sentences below. No matter how incomplete, put down what you can. Try to word the ideas as you understand them in terms of your own life.

1. The problem or need with which the sermon was concerned. *Word it as a question.*

2. The truth developed in the sermon in answer to the question. *Word it as an assertion.*

3. The response to the truth above which the sermon urged. *Word it as an invitation.*

6

Responding to the Sermon

The real value of the sermon lies in what happens inside you. As nice as it is for the preacher to shine in homiletical splendor, his efforts are pretty much worthless apart from your response.

The kind of response you make depends on a number of variables. An obvious factor is your listening skill. If you are faking attention, constantly tuning in and out, yielding to distraction, or stumbling over one of the other barriers to good listening, you are not likely to respond in any meaningful way.

Another factor is your own readiness to respond. I sometimes remind my seminary students that William Carey, the pioneer missionary to India, preached for seven years before he gained his first convert. The people who listened to Carey's fine preaching were simply not ready to respond. To blame a preacher for ineffective sermons may be quite justified; it may, on the other hand, say more about the critics' readiness to respond than the preacher's skill in the pulpit.

Let us say, for the moment, that you do come to the hearing of a sermon with real readiness to respond. Let us say that you listen insightfully and prayerfully. It is not the main idea of the sermon, however, which grips you; it is a striking illustration or a casual comment. What you remember really moves you, and you reorder your life in response to it. Have you then failed to respond properly? Hardly. In theological language, the Holy Spirit has taken the matter out of the preacher's hands and done his work in his own way. The history of preaching and the experience of Christians testify that God's Spirit moves in mysterious ways his wonders to perform. Every preacher knows what it means to step from the pulpit with the glow of having preached a magnificent sermon only to discover that it was a miserable flop in terms of response. He knows too the experience of dejection at having done an abominable job until he hears person after person thank him for having met some pressing personal need.

Judging the effectiveness of a sermon in terms of response alone is a pretty dangerous business. But the preacher does not control response, the Holy Spirit does; the preacher conveys the Bible's message as faithfully as he can and trusts the Holy Spirit to make it real to the hearers in his own way.

All this is not to say that you shouldn't attempt to find the sermon's main idea or to engage in the other suggestions I have made for good listening. It is to say that the combination of your need and the preacher's intention may not always intersect in the expected way; that God may reveal himself through the sermon in a way he chooses.

Having granted that possibility, let us proceed on the assumption that most of the time a good preacher and a good listener will understand what it is God is trying to say through the sermon.

Now, how do you respond to preaching?

The most important response you will make, of course, is the degree to which your behavior will be changed. No preacher expects a radical transformation of everyone's life as the result of every sermon. He does, however, expect some response.

We learned earlier that the three prime purposes of preaching are broadly to evangelize, to teach, and to heal. Your response to the evangelistic sermon may indeed result in the complete transformation of your way of life, as it has for countless persons. If you committed your life to Christ and the church at a previous time, you may respond to such a sermon with a complete blank, feeling that the preacher was talking to someone else. You may respond with a feeling of gratitude that your life is committed to the Christian faith. You may even respond with a determination to share your faith more vigorously now that you have been reminded of its essence and its importance. You may respond meaningfully, you see, even when the sermon appears to be directed to someone else's need.

If the sermon's primary focus is on teaching—the imparting of new information with a view to changed behavior—your response may range from mild interest in the new information to a far-reaching decision which will eventually result in a new set of habits.

The sermon to heal may hit your particular problem directly "on target." You may, for example, receive such new insights on the place of death in God's plan for human life that you resolve almost completely the tensions and anxieties you have felt during the months since a death in your family. That same sermon may mean very little to a teen-ager who has never known anyone close to him to die. For him, the response that is most meaningful is to put the sermon's ideas on the back burner to simmer until needed.

We have been talking about the ultimate, final response which pew-sitters make in response to the sermon. There are some intermediate responses which need looking at too.

OTHER WAYS OF RESPONDING

You may not know it, but your response actually begins with the first word of the sermon. Do you remember the process of communication we talked about in chapter 4? You recall that preaching is a kind of dialogue in which the preacher brings certain meanings to the subject, and you bring meanings out of your life. That same pattern of communication operates at a simpler level too. As the preacher sends out signals in the hope that you will receive them in roughly the way he sends them, you feed back signals which tell him how successful he is. Largely by your facial expression and the movement of your body you communicate an immense amount of information to him.

You may say, without a word, that you are bored with the whole business—perhaps to the point of sleep. You may convey puzzlement and the need for clarification. You may assure him of your agreement with the ideas, probably by a smile or nod of the head. You may indicate disagreement or intense interest without commitment one way or the other. You may, of course, fool him completely by faking attention while you wander mentally.

Naturally, he appreciates most the person who supports him with a smile and other indications of genuine interest.

One of these indications consists of the words you say to him following the service. In many churches the minister makes himself available to greet the parishioners. What you say at this time constitutes a kind of feedback which has the potential of real value. Of relatively little value to him

are the complimentary clichés which come so easily —"I enjoyed your sermon. . . . That was a nice talk. . . . You are a wonderful preacher. . . . What a marvelous sermon."

Preachers do not always know just how to interpret comments like these. Some fall for the flattering words, actually believing the nice things people say about their preaching. Others are cynical, muttering under their breath, "You missed the point; you weren't supposed to *enjoy* it!" Most preachers, I think, realize that people do not have time after the service to reveal their real feelings—or may not know how—but wish to express some kind of appreciation for the inspiration the service has brought them. The only really irritating response, for obvious reasons, is, "You certainly told them off today, pastor!"

If you refer to the sermon at all following the service, and it is not necessary that you do, you do far more good when you say, "Your sermon was so helpful today, pastor—just what I needed. . . . You certainly gave me something to think about. . . . Thank you for a challenging message. . . . You were really talking to me today. . . . I'd like to talk with you sometime about that subject; you've started me thinking." The moments which immediately follow the service are probably not the appropriate time for negative criticism, but you can raise in a conference or a letter the doubts, reservations, or questions which the sermon may have provoked. As long as you do this in a spirit of loving concern—not just to criticize—your clergyman will certainly receive your comments graciously. In fact, he will probably be delighted to know that someone took the sermon seriously enough to respond to it thoughtfully. Your response may even lead to a profitable counseling session in which your pastor can help you to face realistically some problem you have or some question you face.

Discussing the sermon in a group is another way to help you make an intelligent response to preaching. If you are part of a family circle whose other members have also heard the sermon, you may wish to share with each other the insights you have gained as individual listeners.

SERMON FEEDBACK GROUPS

Paralleling the growth of sermon preparation groups in recent years is the development of sermon discussion groups, sometimes called "feedback" groups. I recently asked a religious periodical to run a "help wanted" item in their columns asking readers to write me about their experiences with such groups. Letters came from laymen and ministers all over the country representing every major denomination and some of the smaller ones too. Every one of them said that they had marvelous success with these small gatherings of laymen who came together to discuss the sermon. They seconded the experience of the Institute for Advanced Pastoral Studies in Bloomfield Hills, Michigan, whose alumni have sparked these groups across the country. Some of my students also tried this idea in the churches they serve. For most of them, it has been a revolutionary experience.

For one thing, a sermon discussion group gives you the chance to check your listening efficiency against that of others. When you fill out a set of questions or compare what you have written down as main sermon ideas, you see how accurately you have listened.

Even more important is the way such a group changes your attitude toward the whole business of preaching. My students have found that their sleep-prone members have become interested, alert listeners because they have something to listen for. I have listened to any number of tape-recorded discussion groups in which laymen summarized their experience by saying that they would never again listen quite so casually to a sermon as they had done before. For the rest of their lives they would profit every Sunday from having had to listen carefully and to participate in a feedback group.

An important part of this kind of responding is the way good listeners come increasingly to bring to church the concerns and meanings of their own lives. As they identify themselves with the ideas of the sermons, they sometimes discover meanings that are far deeper and richer even than the preacher intended. They come into encounter with each other at a deeper level than in the normal church program. Through the group experience the saving Word somehow comes to them with a power it never had in their individual, isolated lives.

The preacher himself finds tremendous value in this encounter of his people with the sermon. Whether he participates personally in the discussion or listens to a tape recording of it later in the week, he picks up clues as to the kind of material which gets across (and fails to), the language he uses which may be on the fuzzy side, the mannerisms of speech or action which may be hindering communication, and some sermon topics to be treated later on. Most important to him is the knowledge,

if such groups meet regularly, that at least some of his people will be doing their best to engage in real two-way communication with him. This assurance strengthens him and makes him do his best.

The method of setting up sermon feedback groups varies widely. Generally, a fairly small

group of persons who have been alerted in advance
gather immediately after the worship service for the
discussion, perhaps lubricated by some hot coffee.
If the minister is not there, a tape recording is pro-
vided for him to hear later. In some churches a
youth or adult evening fellowship chews over the
morning sermon. Postponing the discussion to a
midweek service foregoes much of the value because of the rapid rate of forgetting, but may be
the only possibility. If the minister feels that he can
handle the discussion, he may even conclude the
Sunday service a bit early and throw open the discussion to the entire group of persons present.

The Institute for Advanced Pastoral Studies
makes four suggestions growing out of their experience with such groups: (1) the minister should
thoroughly prepare the participants for their task,
especially the dialogical nature of preaching; (2)
the participants should represent a variety of persons in terms of their age and their commitment to
the church (I know one pastor who has an atheist
participate); (3) some laymen feel more free to
discuss if the minister is not present, though they
don't mind tape recording the discussion for him;
(4) participants become more articulate discussants
with practice, but after three or four times tend to

dominate the discussion and thus to discourage newcomers.

Groups should probably number no more than seven or eight and should be continually changing in their membership. To arrange a long-term plan for eventually involving every member of the congregation could be a transforming experience for any church.

Other feedback devices have been tried too. One minister asks a layman to prepare a response to the sermon as a representative of the congregation, to be given from his front seat in the sanctuary before the end of the service. Another invites a panel of three articulate church members to react to the sermon similarly. Still another leaves the back page of the church bulletin blank except for a sentence which indicates that the space is to be used for taking notes during the sermon and jotting down questions or resolutions arising from it. One preacher I know preached the first half of his sermon in which he raised an ethical question frequently faced by the persons in the community. He then announced a text, distributed Bibles, and asked his parishioners to gather in small groups to finish the sermon by discussing the insight of the scripture on the problem. Perhaps the only limiting factors in this method are the ingenuity of the minister and the open-minded-ness of the congregation.

Here is a form you might use in a feedback group.

SERMON FEEDBACK PROJECT

To the participant in the sermon discussion:

The time and effort you bring to this discussion will bring rich dividends both to your pastor and yourself. You will help him evaluate the effectiveness of his preaching, and you will develop your skills in listening. Use the following questions to guide your discussion. You will need between thirty and forty-five minutes to achieve the best results. The discussion will be tape recorded for your pastor to hear later in the week. You will help him most by being frank and honest in your comments. These questions may help you get started.

1. What did this sermon say to you?
2. What difference, if any, do you think the message will make in your life?
3. In what ways did the preacher help or hinder in the presentation of his thought?

THINGS YOU CAN DO

I should like to raise a final question now, and try to provide six simple answers to it—six things you can do. The question is: Besides responding to the specific sermon, what can you do to respond meaningfully to the total preaching ministry of your church?

First, express your honest appreciation frequently for the sermons you hear—even when they leave a lot to be desired. Your preacher is human and needs to feel appreciated.

Second, encourage him to tackle difficult and controversial subjects. Let him know that you are open to hear whatever insights on the knotty problems of modern life he may derive from the written Word of God. He already knows that you may disagree with him; he needs to know that you will support his right to speak as he feels God is speaking to him.

Third, provide ample time and sufficient funds for him to study. See that he has competent secretarial help. Make sure that laymen do the necessary errand-running and administrative detail work which eat so easily into his study time. If he has announced study hours, respect them. Give him a generous allowance for buying books and periodicals.

Fourth, make possible a regular leave of absence for extended study at a theological seminary, university, or center for continuing education. You would be shocked to think that your physician did not take advantage of conferences and seminars to bring him up to date on the latest medical advances. For your clergyman to keep theologically, biblically, and homiletically fresh is fully as important. What's more, the prospect of a biannual or triannual study leave would do much to motivate him to more diligent week-by-week study.

Fifth, make sure that your church is supporting vigorously and generously the program of theological education of your denomination. If ministers in training are going to be really effective preachers, they need highly qualified professors, excellent facilities for study and research, and scholarship money.

Sixth, tell your minister of your willingness to respond to whatever insights God may give you through the preaching of the Word. If you think that means putting yourself on the spot, you're right! Good preaching is a partnership of preacher and listener. He will be delighted with your determination. And so will the One who said, "He who has ears to hear, let him hear."

DESIGN AND ILLUSTRATION: David Dawson
TYPE: Fairfield
    10 pt. leaded 3 pts.

TYPESETTER: The Parthenon Press
MANUFACTURER: The Parthenon Press
PRINTING PROCESS: Letterpress
PAPER: Body, 55 lb. Warren's Novel Antique Special
    White